GRAPHIC MYTHOLOGY
EGYPTIAN MYTHS

by Gary Jeffrey

illustrated by Romano Felmang

The Rosen Publishing Group, Inc., New York

Published in 2006 by The Rosen Publishing Group, Inc.
29 East 21st Street, New York, NY 10010

Copyright © 2006 David West Books

First edition, 2006

Designed and produced by
David West Books

Editor: Dominique Crowley

Photo credits:
    Page 4 bottom, Trevor Spink
    Page 5 top, Vernon Cheng

        Library of Congress Cataloging-in-Publication Data

Jeffrey, Gary.
  Egyptian myths / by Gary Jeffrey ; illustrated by Romano Felmang.
      p. cm. – (Graphic mythology)
  Includes index.
  ISBN 1-4042-0800-3 (library binding) – ISBN 1-4042-0812-7 (pbk.)
–ISBN 1-4042-6252-0 (6 pack)
  1. Mythology, Egyptian – Juvenile literature. I. Felmang, Romano,
ill. II. Title. III. Series.

  BL2441.3.J44 2005
  299'.3113–dc22

                                                2005017641

Manufactured in China

CONTENTS

GODS AND KINGS

Ancient Egypt was one of the first great civilizations on Earth. Over the course of 3,500 years, the ancient Egyptians created a rich mythology of stories that expressed their culture, lifestyle, and religion.

RISE OF THE PHARAOH

The first Egyptians came from central Africa and settled in the fertile river valley of the Nile. Each year, rains in the south would bring floods to the valleys. The rich silt that settled on the banks made the soil healthy. This allowed the people to farm successfully.

No one knows how Tutankhamen, the eighteen-year-old pharaoh, died.

As the civilization flourished, the country became two separate kingdoms — Upper Egypt in the south and Lower Egypt in the north. Around 3118 B.C., Upper Egypt was ruled by King Menes. He conquered Lower Egypt and was the first Egyptian pharaoh to rule the entire land. The pharaohs, who were very powerful, were seen by the Egyptian people as gods on Earth. To honor them, the Egyptians built amazing statues to house their bodies and possessions when they died.

Scientists and historians are still debating how the Egyptians built the pyramids.

Ancient Egyptians used picture symbols called hieroglyphics as a written language.

ANCIENT TEXTS

The ancient Egyptians used a set of signs to pass on their myths from older people to younger ones. These symbols are called hieroglyphics and were written on the walls of pharaohs' tombs. Pyramid Texts were special writings on pharaohs' coffins. They were instructions to guide dead kings through the underworld and gain immortality. Eventually, they were written on papyrus scrolls and collected into a book called *The Book of the Dead.*

MYTHICAL MEANINGS

Like other ancient cultures, Egyptians used myths to make sense of their world. Stories about life after death, for example, helped them to understand the yearly renewal of their farmland after the flooding of the Nile. Every year, the land would become dry and lifeless because of the hot Egyptian sun. When the rain came, the soil was renewed and people were able to grow crops. Stories about the world around them gave meaning to Egyptians' lives.

Egyptian gods took many forms. For example, Bastet, goddess of mothers, was often shown as a cat.

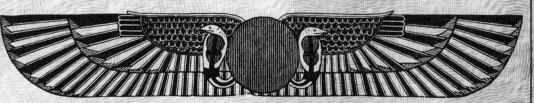

This solar disk is a symbol of the sun god. It is used on jewelry and temple doorways from ancient Egypt.

THREE EGYPTIAN MYTHS

The following three stories were famous in ancient Egypt. The first is a creation myth, while the second tells a tale of betrayal and death. In the final myth, there is a fierce battle between good and evil.

THE STORY OF RA

This story comes from the ancient city of Heliopolis in Upper Egypt. Heliopolis was the center of worship for the sun god, Ra. Ra was one of the first gods. He was greatly admired by the Egyptians.

Ra
Ra, the sun god, is linked to light and heat. His symbol is the solar disk, which he wears on top of the head of a hawk. Ra changes his form to become different shapes.

Thoth
Thoth is Ra's son and the god of wisdom and learning. He wears the head of the ibis (a sacred Egyptian bird). Often, the ibis' head is under a moon-shaped disk.

Apophis
Apophis is the chief demon of the night. He is a deadly serpent who attacks others with mists. His mission is to destroy Ra and prevent the sunrise each morning.

OSIRIS AND ISIS

Osiris was one of the most popular gods in Egypt. He taught people about farming, showing them how to grow crops and live off the land. Egyptians use the myth of Osiris and Isis to explain how they became one of the first great civilizations.

Osiris
Osiris is the first Egyptian ruler who was also a god. He is shown as a green-skinned monarch when dead (page 35).

Isis
As a goddess and the wife of Osiris, Isis symbolizes the perfect woman. The ancient Egyptians called her the great mother.

Seth
Seth is Osiris' brother and is known as the red god. He has a violent and jealous temper. Seth is associated with the desert and storms.

HORUS FIGHTS SETH

The myth of Horus' fight with Seth takes place over many years. It involves enormous armies and many battles. In this story, Horus battles with the evil desert god, Seth, to punish him for killing Horus' father, Osiris.

Ra-Herakhti
Ra-Herakhti is an earthly incarnation of Ra. In early mythology he is shown as a king, and is linked to the horizon.

Horus
Isis' son is first seen as a young warrior and then as a hawk-headed god. Horus is known as the protector of kings.

Seth
In this book, Seth is at war with Ra for control of the land. He appears in a variety of disguises – including a red hippo.

THE STORY OF RA

AS THE BOAT CLIMBS UPWARD, KHEPRI'S RADIANCE GROWS STRONGER.

AT THE HEIGHT OF HIS POWER KHEPRI BECOMES *RA* – THE SUN GOD.

AS THE DAY WEARS ON, RA'S POWER BEGINS TO FADE. HE CHANGES INTO A HUMAN FORM, CALLED *ATUM*. AS THEY DROP BEHIND THE WESTERN MOUNTAINS, THEY PREPARE TO ENTER...

...*TUAT*, THE UNDERWORLD.

THE DARK KINGDOM IS APPROACHING FAST!

FEAR NOT! WE ARE READY FOR **THEM.**

THEM: THE LEGION OF DEVILS THAT SPRANG FROM THE DARKNESS.
BEWARE! THE GREAT SNAKE LEADS THE CHARGE!
HIISSSSSSSSSSSSS!
WATCH OUT! HE SPRAYS BLACK MIST!!!
WE CAN'T DEFEAT HIM!!
THE SERPENT'S NAME IS APOPHIS. THIS FIERCE NIGHT-DEMON ATTACKS THE BOAT...
ATUM STEPS IN.
PHWUMMM!
FEEL THE POWER OF MY DEADLY SUNBOLTS!

...ATUM CHANGES INTO A CAT...

YEEEEOOOOW!

...AND FINALLY KILLS APOPHIS.

THAK!

THE SERPENT'S BODY IS CHOPPED INTO A HUNDRED PIECES. HIS BLOOD STAINS THE EVENING SKY.

TRIUMPHANT, RA RISES TO LIGHT ANOTHER DAY.

THE END

OSIRIS AND ISIS

IN ANCIENT TIMES, EGYPT WAS KNOWN AS A DANGEROUS PLACE. PEOPLE WOULD TEAR EACH OTHER APART AND RIP BODIES LIMB FROM LIMB TO FEAST ON **HUMAN FLESH!**

GRRRAAAAGH!

THEN ONE DAY OSIRIS WAS BORN.

BEHOLD! THE LORD OF ALL COMES FORTH TO THE LIGHT!

OSIRIS, BORN OF THE GODDESS, NUT, BECOMES THE FIRST KING OF EGYPT. HE TEACHES THE PEOPLE HOW TO FARM THE LAND, HONOR THE GODS, AND OBEY HIS FAIR LAWS.

17

THE COFFIN, NOW THE TOMB OF OSIRIS, IS CARRIED FROM THE PALACE.

TO THE RIVER!

HEAVE!

SPLOSH!

THE WATERS OF THE NILE CARRY THE COFFIN FAR AWAY TO THE SEA.

FAREWELL BROTHER – FOREVER!

IT TRAVELS UNTIL IT REACHES THE SHORES OF BYBLOS, WHERE A GREAT WAVE SWEEPS IT ONTO THE TOP OF A TAMARISK TREE.

SWOOOOSH!

AS THE WATER DRAWS BACK, THE TREE'S BRANCHES CIRCLE AROUND THE COFFIN. THEY PULL THE COFFIN DOWN INTO THE DEPTHS OF THE TREE'S TRUNK.

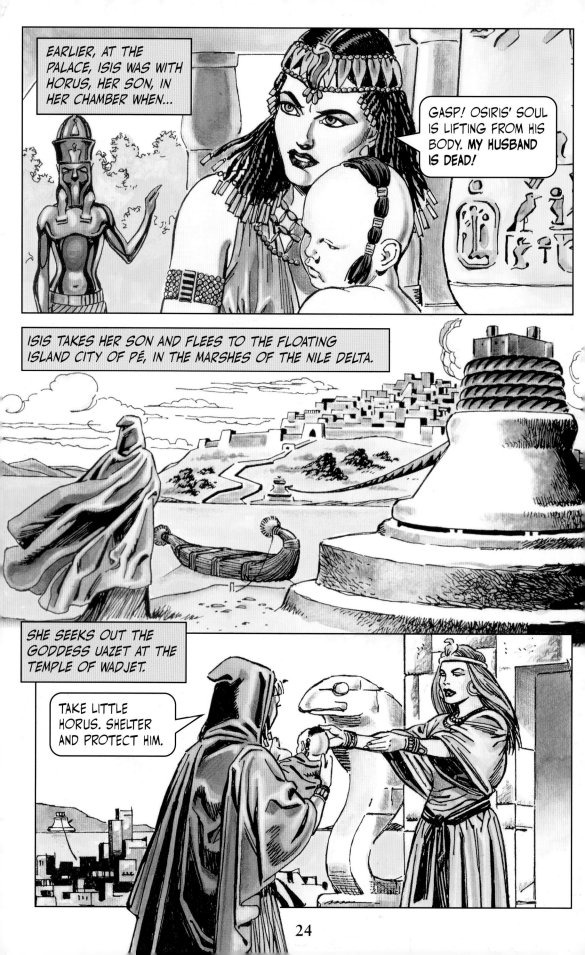

WHERE ARE YOU GOING?

TO FIND THE BODY OF MY HUSBAND.

CRACKK!

WHEN SHE REACHES THE MAINLAND, ISIS USES HER MAGIC TO CUT THE ROPES THAT HOLD THE ISLANDS TOGETHER.

GO! FAR AWAY! WHERE SETH WILL **NEVER** FIND YOU!

MEANWHILE, KING MALKANDER AND QUEEN ATHENIS OF BYBLOS ARE WALKING BY THE SEASHORE OF BYBLOS. THEY SEE THE TREE THAT HOLDS OSIRIS' BODY.

I WILL HAVE IT MADE INTO A BEAUTIFUL PILLAR TO DECORATE YOUR CHAMBER!

LOOK AT THIS TREE! HAVE YOU EVER SEEN A FINER ONE?!

NEVER!

THE MAIDENS SIT WITH ISIS AND ALLOW HER TO BRAID THEIR HAIR. THE WHOLE TIME, SHE BREATHES A SWEET SCENT ON THEM.

WHEN THEY RETURN TO THE PALACE, THEY ARE MET BY QUEEN ATHENIS.

WHAT IS THAT WONDERFUL SMELL?

IT'S FROM THE SAD LADY WHO WAITS BY THE SHORE.

ATHENIS CALLS ISIS TO THE PALACE.

WHY ARE YOU SO SAD?

I MISS MY SON, HORUS.

I HAVE A SON, TOO, BUT HE IS SICK.

COME! YOU MUST TAKE ME TO HIM!

A FEW MOMENTS LONGER AND ALL THAT IS MORTAL IN HIM WOULD HAVE BURNED AWAY. HE WOULD HAVE BEEN A GOD!

EVEN THOUGH ATHENIS DISTURBED THE HEALING SPELL, DIKTYS IS BETTER AND THE KING IS VERY HAPPY.

ISIS, YOU CAN HAVE ANYTHING IN THE KINGDOM. JUST NAME IT AND IT'S YOURS.

GIVE ME WHAT THAT PILLAR HOLDS AND I WILL BE CONTENT.

KING MALKANDER ORDERS THAT THE PILLAR BE CUT OPEN.

THWAK!

SPLINTER!

OSIRIS, MY LOVE!

HAVING TAKEN OUT OSIRIS' BODY, THE PILLAR IS TAKEN DOWN AND WRAPPED IN FINE LINEN. ISIS SPRINKLES SWEET SPICES AND BLOSSOMS ON IT AND RETURNS IT TO THE ROYAL COUPLE.

ISIS TAKES OSIRIS' BODY HOME TO EGYPT.

IN A QUIET PLACE, SHE OPENS THE COFFIN.

DEAR HUSBAND, YOU WHO ONCE RULED THE LIVING...

...ARE NOW KING OF THE DEAD.

ISIS REPLACES THE LID AND HIDES THE COFFIN CAREFULLY. THEN, SHE SETS OFF TO FIND THE CITY OF PÉ AND HORUS.

THIS TIME, ISIS SETS OUT IN A PAPYRUS BOAT. SHE IS HELPED BY ALL THE ANIMALS OF THE WILD.

EACH TIME SHE FINDS A PIECE OF OSIRIS BODY, ISIS PRETENDS TO BURY IT. SHE MAKES A SHRINE TO MARK THE PLACE.

THIS IS DONE TO **DECEIVE** SETH WHILE SHE SECRETLY PIECES OSIRIS BACK TOGETHER AGAIN.

HUSBAND, I HAVE MADE YOU **WHOLE** BUT I CANNOT MAKE YOU **LIVE**. ONLY OUR VENGEANCE CAN DO THAT.

UNTIL THEN, OSIRIS CONTINUES TO RULE IN TUAT, *THE KINGDOM OF THE DEAD.*

THE END

35

HORUS FIGHTS SETH

DURING THE 363RD YEAR OF HIS REIGN ON EARTH, THE GOD RA-HERAKHTI BRINGS HIS ARMY TO NUBIA FOR A MAJOR BATTLE AGAINST THE EVIL GOD, SETH.

TODAY COULD BE OUR DAY FOR VICTORY. ARE YOU READY, HORUS?

AS YOU KNOW, I WOULD GIVE A **DAY** OF FEASTING FOR JUST ONE HOUR OF FIGHTING !

THE YOUNG GOD, HORUS, IS ONE OF RA'S MOST EAGER LIEUTENANTS.

AND WHAT WOULD YOU GIVE FOR THE CHANCE TO AVENGE YOUR FATHER?

ANYTHING!

SETH HAD KILLED HORUS' FATHER, OSIRIS, YEARS BEFORE. HIS MOTHER, ISIS, HAD SWORN HER SON WOULD SEEK VENGEANCE.

SUDDENLY, SETH'S MEN CANNOT RECOGNIZE ONE ANOTHER.

THOUGH THEY SHOUT, THEY ARE UNABLE TO UNDERSTAND EACH OTHER'S WORDS.

THINKING THE ENEMY IS AMONG THEM, THEY **PANIC** AND START ATTACKING EACH OTHER.

WHILE THE SOLDIERS OF SETH'S ADVANCE GUARD WIPE THEMSELVES OUT, RA'S ARMY RUSHES FORWARD. MEANWHILE, HORUS IS SEEKING **SETH.**

WHERE ARE YOU? WHERE ARE YOU?

THERE! AT THE REAR!

AS THE TWO SIDES MEET, HORUS DIVES IN.

RED GOD! YOUR TIME ON EARTH IS NEARLY OVER!

WHEN HORUS CATCHES UP WITH SETH, SETH HAS CHANGED BACK INTO HIS HUMAN FORM.

BOUFFFF!

WHACK!

WHERE ARE YOU GOING?

I HAVE IT!

IT'S TIME THIS BATTLE WAS FINISHED!

HORUS EQUIPS HIMSELF WITH A HARPOON.

MORE MYTHICAL CHARACTERS

Many gods other than the Great Nine are featured in Egyptian myths.

ABUTU-FISH — A mythical fish that appears with Ra's boat at sunrise.

AMUN — Amun is the god of the wind. Usually, he is shown wearing a crown with two large feathers in it. Amun becomes very important when joined to Ra. As Amun-Ra he is the supreme god of Egypt.

ANUBIS — Anubis is associated with funerals and mummies. He has the head of a jackal, a type of dog. Anubis was the first to cover the dead in a protective liquid that kept the bodies fresh. This is a process called embalming. He also guards the dead in their tombs.

BES — This little fat dwarf is known as the god of dance, music, and pleasure. His job is to make children happy. Often, he is seen with a curly beard.

HATHOR — An important goddess of love and fertility, Hathor is often shown as a cow, or sometimes as a woman wearing a headdress. She becomes Sakhmet, goddess of war and destiny, after Ra sends her to destroy people on Earth.

KHNUM — A creator god whose name means "the molder." Usually, he is drawn with a human head and sheep's body, making people on a potter's wheel. He is believed to be a protector of the Nile river.

KHONSU — The god of the moon and time, Khonsu is thought to have magical powers that could drive out evil spirits from humans. Many works of Egyptian art show him as a mummy with a curved moon resting above his head.

MONTU — Montu is linked to winning wars. He is close friends with Amun and, later, becomes his adopted son. Montu is often shown with a hawk's head. He has a sacred bull, which is believed to be the soul of Ra.

MUT — Mut is the mother-goddess of all other goddesses. She wears either a vulture headdress or a lion headdress. Mut is married to Amun-Ra and is the queen of heaven.

PTAH — This god is thought to be the designer of the universe. He holds a long, special stick, called a scepter, and is shown as a mummy. Everything on Earth is thought to have been made by him. Ptah is so important that some people believe that other gods are Ptah in a different form. Some small communities, such as the one at Memphis, also saw him as the god of artists.

SAKHMET — A close friend of Ptah, she is the goddess of war and battles. She begins life as Hathor, but changes to Sakhmet when she destroys all of Ra's enemies. Her name means "the powerful one." She is seen as a woman with the head of a lioness.

SOBEK — Sobek is known as the crocodile god because of his crocodile appearance. He is the god of fertility, both of people and their crops. He is also associated with water.

SHU — This god of the air is one of a pair of gods whose job it is to hold up the sky above Earth. He is often shown with an ostrich feather on his head.

TEFNUT — Tefnut is the twin sister of Shu. She keeps the sky above Earth with him. She has the head of a lioness. In early stories, she is the goddess of the moon. In later tales, she is the goddess of dew and rain.

WADJET — This goddess keeps Lower Egypt safe. Wadjet is shown as a type of snake called a cobra. She has wings and a red crown. At other times, she is seen as a woman wearing a red crown and holding a scepter.

GLOSSARY

advance guard A group of soldiers who travel ahead of the main group of soldiers in an army.

avenge To take satisfaction in punishing a wrongdoer.

awe To feel a great sense of wonder at something.

chaos Something in a complete mess.

deceive To be false or lie on purpose.

delta The place where a river meets the sea.

duel A fight between two people.

eclipse When a moon, a star, or a planet hides all or part of another.

epic A very long poem about a hero.

eternal When something will last forever.

fertile To produce plants or crops plentifully.

flourish To grow and be successful.

harpoon Sharp spear used to kill animals.

hieroglyphics A type of Egyptian writing that uses pictures and symbols in place of words.

incarnation When a god appears in human form.

inform To give someone knowledge.

linen Light woven fabric, usually made from the flax plant.

mortal A being who will die eventually. Humans are mortal, but gods are immortal because they live forever.

papyrus A type of paper made from the papyrus plant.

pharaoh An ancient Egyptian ruler.

reign The period of time that a person, such as a king or queen, rules a country.

rouse To wake up.

rudder A flat piece of wood attached to the back of a boat. When the rudder is turned, the boat changes direction.

silt A type of mud that has lots of food for plants in it.

swallow A small bird that has a short beak and long pointed wings. It catches insects to eat while it is flying.

tamarisk tree A shrub or small tree, with feathery leaves and pink or white blossom, found in the Mediterranean and central Asia.

thicket A thick group of plants or bushes.

tragedy A very sad story in which the main character dies.

underworld The place where souls go after bodies have died.

FOR MORE INFORMATION

ORGANIZATIONS

Egyptian Museum and Planetarium
1342 Naglee Ave
San Jose, CA 95191
(408) 947-3635
Web site: http://www.egyptianmuseum.org/index.html

Fine Arts Museums of San Francisco
Legion of Honor
34th Avenue & Clement Street
Lincoln Park
San Francisco, CA 94121
(415) 750-3600
Web site: http://www.thinker.org/legion/

FOR FURTHER READING

Jeffrey, Gary and Anita Ganeri. *Cleopatra. Life of an Egyptian Queen.*
New York, NY: Rosen Publishing Group, Inc., 2005.

Lancelyn Green, Roger and Heather Copely. *Tales of Ancient Egypt.*
New York, NY: Penguin Putnam Books for Young Readers, 2004.

Morgan, Julian. *Cleopatra: Ruling in the Shadow of Rome.* New York,
NY: Rosen Publishing Group, Inc., 2003.

Payne, Elizabeth. *The Pharaohs of Ancient Egypt.* NY: Random House
Books,1981.

Tarr, Judith. *Throne of Isis.* New York, NY: Tom Doherty Associates,
1994.

INDEX

Web Sites

Due to the changing nature of Internet links, the Rosen Publishing Group, Inc., has developed an online list of Web sites related to the subject of this book. This site is updated regularly. Please use this link to access the list:

http://www.rosenlinks.com/gm/egyptian